WITHDRAWN FROM LIBRARY

BUILDING BY DESIGN

ENGINEERING
THE PANAMA CANAL

BY YVETTE LaPIERRE

CONTENT CONSULTANT
William Ibbs, PhD
University of California at Berkeley
Ibbs Consulting

Cover image: A ship enters one of Panama Canal's locks.

Core Library

An Imprint of Abdo Publishing
abdopublishing.com

abdopublishing.com

Published by Abdo Publishing, a division of ABDO, PO Box 398166, Minneapolis, Minnesota 55439. Copyright © 2018 by Abdo Consulting Group, Inc. International copyrights reserved in all countries. No part of this book may be reproduced in any form without written permission from the publisher. Core Library™ is a trademark and logo of Abdo Publishing.

Printed in the United States of America, North Mankato, Minnesota
082017
012018

THIS BOOK CONTAINS RECYCLED MATERIALS

Cover Photo: iStockphoto
Interior Photos: iStockphoto, 1; De Agostini/Getty Images, 4–5; Peter Hermes Furian/Shutterstock Images, 6; Bettmann/Getty Images, 9, 17, 27, 33; AP Images, 12–13, 29; Moffett Studio/Library of Congress, 15; Time Life Pictures/Panama Canal Photo/The LIFE Images Collection/Getty Images, 19; Claus Lunau/Science Source, 20; Buyenlarge/Archive Photos/Getty Images, 24–25, 43; Galina Savina/Shutterstock Images, 36–37, 45; Arnulfo Franco/AP Images, 39

Editor: Arnold Ringstad
Imprint Designer: Maggie Villaume
Series Design Direction: Laura Polzin

Publisher's Cataloging-in-Publication Data

Names: LaPierre, Yvette, author.
Title: Engineering the Panama Canal / by Yvette LaPierre.
Description: Minneapolis, Minnesota : Abdo Publishing, 2018. | Series: Building by design | Includes online resources and index.
Identifiers: LCCN 2017946987 | ISBN 9781532113758 (lib.bdg.) | ISBN 9781532152634 (ebook)
Subjects: LCSH: Panama Canal (Panama)--Juvenile literature. | Canals--Panama--Juvenile literature. | Building--Juvenile literature.
Classification: DDC 972.875--dc23
LC record available at https://lccn.loc.gov/2017946987

CONTENTS

CHAPTER ONE
A Plan to Move Mountains **4**

CHAPTER TWO
Starting and Stopping **12**

CHAPTER THREE
Make the Dirt Fly **24**

CHAPTER FOUR
The Panama Canal Today **36**

Fast Facts **42**

Stop and Think **44**

Glossary **46**

Online Resources **47**

Learn More **47**

Index **48**

About the Author **48**

CHAPTER ONE

A PLAN TO MOVE MOUNTAINS

President Woodrow Wilson pressed a small button in Washington, DC, in October 1913. It sent a signal thousands of miles through telegraph wires. The signal went all the way to Central America. When it reached Panama, it exploded a dam holding back a river. The river flooded a canal linking the Atlantic and Pacific Oceans. With the press of a button, world trade suddenly became much faster.

Until then, the trip from the Atlantic to the Pacific was long and dangerous. Ships

A newspaper illustration from 1913 depicts the moment Wilson sent the signal to Panama.

ISTHMUS OF PANAMA

The Isthmus of Panama links North and South America. It is about 50 miles (81 km) across. It is the narrowest strip of land between the Atlantic Ocean and the Pacific Ocean. Why might the canal have been built there? Are there other good places the canal could have been built?

had to sail around the southern tip of South America. Yet a narrow strip of land separated the two oceans by just 50 miles (81 km). This was the Isthmus of Panama. Explorers and sailors had long dreamed of a water shortcut here. This would make journeys much shorter.

The French were the first to attempt to build a canal across Panama. They began work in 1880. Their plan involved digging a canal at sea level. The French struggled due to mistakes and a lack of funds. Diseases killed many workers. France stopped the project in 1889.

THE PANAMA RAILWAY

Gold was discovered in California in the 1840s. Thousands of people traveled there in search of riches. Some made the long trip around the tip of South America by ship. Others slowly crossed North America by wagon. Some US businessmen decided to build a railway across Panama as a shortcut. It was finished in 1855. Engineers planning the route found something important. They noticed a gap in the ridge of tall mountains at a place called Culebra. This would eventually provide a path for the Panama Canal.

PANAMA CANAL TREATY

In 1902, the United States bought the old French canal project for $40 million. At the time, Panama belonged to Colombia. The United States needed a treaty with Colombia to begin building. But Colombian officials thought the treaty was unfair. They refused to sign it. Some Panamanians were in favor of the canal treaty. They wanted independence from Colombia. They planned a rebellion. President Theodore Roosevelt supported them. He sent two US gunboats to Panama's harbor. They didn't allow Colombian troops to land. Colombian troops were unable to reach the rebellion to stop it. Panama gained independence on November 3, 1903. Days later, the United States signed a treaty with the new Republic of Panama.

The United States paid Panama $10 million for the land. It stretched 10 miles (16 km) wide from coast to coast along the route where the canal would be

Roosevelt believed in showing off US military strength to achieve the nation's goals.

PERSPECTIVES
GUNBOAT DIPLOMACY

Many people were unhappy with Roosevelt's actions at the time. They did not like that he sent gunboats to Panama. Newspapers called it land grabbing. Roosevelt defended his actions. He denied that he helped the rebellion. He wrote a special message to Congress. He argued that all people would benefit from the canal. Some people supported Roosevelt, including Congress. It voted in favor of the canal.

built. It was called the Canal Zone. American engineers and laborers from around the world spent the next ten years building the Panama Canal. They excavated entire mountains to connect two oceans. It was the largest construction project of its time. It was also a triumph of engineering.

STRAIGHT TO THE SOURCE

On January 4, 1904, Roosevelt wrote a special message to Congress. In it, he defended his actions in Panama:

> *I confidently maintain that the recognition of the Republic of Panama was an act justified by the interests of collective civilization. If ever a government could be said to have received a mandate from civilization to effect an object the accomplishment of which was demanded in the interest of mankind, the United States holds that position with regard to the interoceanic canal.*
>
> Source: "Theodore Roosevelt Special Message, January 4, 1904." *The American Presidency Project*. The American Presidency Project, n.d. Web. Accessed April 25, 2017.

Point of View

Roosevelt argues that the canal was necessary for all people. Why might he have thought this? Read back through the chapter. Do you think Roosevelt was right? Why or why not?

CHAPTER TWO

STARTING AND STOPPING

John Wallace was the US project's first chief engineer. He arrived in Panama in June 1904. He found a mess. Piles of machinery lay rusting. Buildings were falling down. Railroads were worn out. The dirt streets were deep in mud and sewage. But he also found an 11-mile (18-km) canal. It was 25 feet (8 m) deep and 70 feet (21 m) wide. The French had already moved some 30 million cubic yards (23 million cubic m) of dirt.

Wallace got to work right away. He continued to dig the sea-level canal the French

Progress on the canal was slow in 1904.

had started. It was frustrating work. He didn't have the right tools. Workers didn't have proper housing and food. There was no final design for the canal. And diseases continued to kill many in the Canal Zone. After a year, he left. New chief engineer John Stevens arrived in July 1905. He ordered a stop to the digging. He realized that there was no point in continuing until everything was ready. For the next year, he focused on disease control, infrastructure, and the canal plan. Stevens also had to deal with heavy rainfall and drainage problems.

MOSQUITO CONTROL

More than 20,000 workers died from disease during the French building phase. The main diseases were yellow fever and malaria. Stevens realized that the canal could not be built if the workers were not safe. Dr. William Gorgas was hired to tackle disease in the Canal Zone.

Stevens had decades of experience in civil engineering when he arrived at the canal.

PERSPECTIVES
MOSQUITOES AND DISEASE

Gorgas's job was to make the Canal Zone safer for people. He had caught yellow fever when he was a young man. He survived. After that, yellow fever became his specialty. He spent many years studying how mosquitoes passed diseases to humans. He knew that yellow fever and malaria were carried by two different kinds of mosquitoes. He also knew the best way to prevent these diseases. It was to control the mosquitoes that spread them. At the time, this was a new approach to disease prevention. Gorgas's work in Panama made the canal possible.

Stevens gave him a big budget. He assigned thousands of workers to him.

Gorgas's plan was to focus on the mosquitos that carry these diseases. His workers sprayed insecticide in houses and buildings. They put screens in windows. Mosquitoes lay eggs in still water, so they removed all containers that collected water. They sprayed the surfaces of ponds and puddles with oil. That killed the mosquito larvae. It was the biggest disease program ever seen. It worked.

Gorgas, a US Army doctor, oversaw the draining of swamps and other anti-mosquito efforts.

Within 18 months, yellow fever was gone in Panama. The number of malaria cases dropped.

INFRASTRUCTURE

The canal workers needed homes, clean water, and good food. Stevens began work on new houses. He oversaw the building of hospitals, schools, and churches. He worked on roads and sewage systems. New pipes delivered clean running water. Railroads were repaired. They could now be used to deliver fresh food and supplies.

Railroads would also help with digging. There was no point in excavating tons of earth if it couldn't be moved quickly. Stevens replaced the existing narrow railroad tracks with wide ones. The wide tracks could carry the huge new trains he ordered from the United States. He also had double tracks laid. That way trains could go both directions at once. Steam shovels would dump their loads of dirt into an empty railcar. When full, the railcar could head to either end of the canal. In the meantime, an empty car would roll into place. This would make digging go much more quickly.

DESIGN

Stevens needed one last thing before building: a final design. When the Americans took over the canal

Large crews built and maintained the railroads needed for the canal construction.

PANAMA CANAL
PLAN

The Panama Canal continues to work as planned today. Ships enter through bays at either end of the canal. A series of locks lift the ship 85 feet (26 m) to the level of Gatun Lake. The lake was formed by damming the Chagres River. Ships cross the lake and sail through a channel cut through the mountains. This is the Culebra Cut. On the other side, locks lower the ship back down to sea level. Can you imagine what the canal would look like if it were a sea-level canal?

in 1904, the plan was to continue with the original sea-level canal. A sea-level canal connects two bodies of water on one level. But others argued that a lock canal would be better. Lock canals have more than one level. The locks move ships up and down, like water stairs. There were two major obstacles to both plans. The first was the miles of tall mountains across the isthmus. The second was the wild Chagres River. The river regularly flooded. It caused huge landslides.

Some argued for the sea-level canal. They said it could be

BUILDING TOOLS

Engineers used the latest technologies in the canal. One of the most important tools was the Bucyrus steam shovel. This was the biggest steam shovel available. It weighed about 95 tons (86 metric tons). It could move earth three times faster than the shovels used by the French. At the height of digging, more than 100 of the Bucyrus steam shovels ate away at the mountains. Other machines were invented specifically for use on the canal. One was a machine to spread excavated dirt. Another was a crane that moved huge railroad tracks. Explosives were also important tools.

widened more easily as ships grew bigger. And no one had ever built locks of the size needed for this project. They might not work or be safe. But Stevens argued that a lock canal would take much less digging. The lock plan had another benefit. It included a huge dam on the Chagres River. The dam would control the river. It would stop the river from flooding and destroying the canal. Stevens persuaded Roosevelt and Congress. In 1906, two years after beginning the project, the Americans had a final plan. But the next year, Stevens quit. He never disclosed the reason he left the project.

STRAIGHT TO THE SOURCE

In early 1906, John Stevens went to Washington, DC. There, he successfully argued for a lock canal plan:

The sum of my conclusions is, therefore, that, all things considered, the lock type or high-level canal is preferable to the sea-level type, so called, for the following reasons: It will provide a safer and quicker passage for ships, and therefore, will be of greater capacity. It will provide, beyond question, the best solution of the vital problem of how safely to care for the floodwaters of the Chagres and other streams. Provision is made for enlarging its capacity to almost any extent at very less expense in time and money than can be provided by any sea-level plan. Its cost of operation, maintenance and fixed charges will be much less than any sea-level canal.

Source: John Frank Stevens. *An Engineer's Recollections.* New York: McGraw-Hill, 1936. Print. 41.

Back It Up

Stevens uses evidence, rather than opinions, to support his argument for a lock-type canal. Write a paragraph describing the point he is making. Then write down two or three pieces of evidence he uses to make the point.

CHAPTER THREE

MAKE THE DIRT FLY

A lock canal would mean much less digging. The cut through the mountains no longer had to be dug down to sea level. This would save time and money. But it would also be more complicated than the sea-level plan. George Goethals took over as chief engineer in 1907. It would be up to him to carry out the canal's construction. He directed the three most important tasks. The first was building the Gatun Dam. Next was digging the cut through the mountains. The last big task was building the locks on each end of the canal.

Men, equipment, and rubble filled the Canal Zone during the years of digging.

GATUN DAM

The final plan called for a huge earthen dam across the Chagres River shortly before it emptied into the Atlantic Ocean. Gatun Dam would accomplish three things. First, it would tame the wild river. The Chagres swelled during rainy times. It caused terrible floods and mudslides that could ruin a canal. Second, the dam would create a calm lake for ships to cross above sea level. Third, the lake would provide much of the water needed for the locks.

The first step was to clear the site of its thick jungle cover. Then two rock walls were built across the river valley. They were about 0.25 miles (0.4 km) apart. Next, workers filled the gap between the walls with dirt and small rocks. Then they poured in a soupy mixture of clay and mud. As the mixture dried, it became hard as cement. The dam had to be strong enough to hold back the huge lake. In the center of the dam, engineers built a concrete spillway. The spillway was 100 feet (30.5 m) high and 800 feet (244 m) across. Steel gates were set into the concrete. They could open and close like

By forming Gatun Lake, which gives ships a route across the isthmus, Gatun Dam makes the canal possible.

windows. The gates would safely control the flow of water from Gatun Lake.

When finished in 1914, Gatun Dam was the biggest earthen dam in the world. It was 6,400 feet (1,951 m) long and 2,300 feet (701 m) wide at its base. It rose 110 feet (33.5 m). The Chagres River backed up for miles behind the dam. It created Gatun Lake. It was the largest artificial lake at the time. The new lake was 164 square miles (425 sq km) in area. Its rising waters covered entire villages. Approximately 20,000 people were forced to resettle elsewhere.

CULEBRA CUT

Tall mountains stood between Gatun Lake and the Pacific Ocean. A channel had to be cut through them. The Culebra Cut was only 9 miles (14.5 km) long. But it was the hardest and most dangerous part of the canal project.

Steam shovels worked in the cut all day. They dug 8 tons (7.3 metric tons) of spoil in a single scoop. Spoil is dirt and rock removed in the process of digging. Shovels dumped the spoil into waiting trains. The trains

Roosevelt himself came to inspect progress on the Culebra Cut. His visit to Panama made him the first sitting president to travel abroad.

PERSPECTIVES
UNEQUAL TREATMENT

People came from all over the world to work on the canal. Some came from the United States and Europe. Others traveled from Asia and Latin America. Many came from the small island of Barbados. White Americans and Europeans had nice houses with screens on the windows. They had good schools and hospitals. They were paid well. Other workers were given small, cramped houses without running water. Schools for their children were in run-down buildings. They had few teachers or books. West Indians from Barbados were given the most dangerous jobs. They were poorly paid. They were also much more likely to die from accidents and disease.

carried the spoil to other parts of the canal. Much of the spoil was used to build Gatun Dam. Workers drilled holes deep into the rock. They packed the holes with dynamite. The blasting was done at night when most workers were not around. But no matter how careful they were, accidents injured and killed many men.

Mudslides slowed the progress during the rainy season. Acres of mud and rock slid down the steep sides of the cut. The mud buried steam shovels. It tore up railway tracks. Mudslides could destroy months of digging in one day. As the channel grew deeper, the mudslides got worse. Engineers decided they needed to make the channel wider and its slopes less steep. It meant more digging. But the gently sloping sides were more stable than steep sides. When completed, the cut was 300 feet (91 m) wide. It was more than 250 feet (76 m) deep in some places. In all, workers dug 2 million cubic yards (1.5 million cubic m) of dirt to create the Culebra Cut.

LOCKS

The plan called for huge concrete locks. Engineers had built locks before, but never ones so big. The locks would be the largest concrete structures ever built. Each end of the canal would have three pairs of locks. The locks were built in pairs so they could handle two lanes of traffic. The six sets of locks would take six years to build.

The first two years were spent excavating. Much of the work was done by dredges. A dredge is a machine that scoops up earth from the bottom of a river or lake. The spoil was used to help fill Gatun Dam. Next, the concrete floors and walls were poured. A system of steel towers, giant cranes, and overhead cables was built for the job. It was used to deliver, mix, and pour the cement. Cranes or cables lifted 6-ton (5-metric ton) buckets of concrete and poured them into steel forms. The walls of each lock were 1,000 feet (305 m) long and 81 feet (25 m) high. That's like a giant box nearly five city blocks long with six-story buildings for sides.

Concrete swells and shrinks as it warms and cools. This meant that workers couldn't pour it all in one huge piece. Instead, they poured it in a giant checkerboard pattern. After some squares hardened, they filled the open spaces. This process prevented the concrete from cracking.

Railroad tracks ran straight through the lock construction site, carrying materials and equipment.

HYDROELECTRIC POWER

Few homes or buildings in the United States had electricity at the time the canal project was started. Despite that, engineers wanted to use hydroelectric power to help build and operate the canal. They built a power plant next to the Gatun Dam spillway. Water pouring over the spillway from Gatun Lake hit giant turbines. That caused the turbines to spin, generating electricity. The electricity was used to run all the locks. It also powered cranes, cement mixers, and other machines. Homes and buildings in the Canal Zone had electric lights. The new field of electrical engineering benefited from the advances made while building the canal.

Steel gates formed each end of the locks. The gates swung open and closed like double doors. Each door weighed several hundred tons. Tunnels and pipes carried water to the lock. Valves controlled the water flowing through the pipes. Gravity powered the flow of water. When a valve was opened at the upper end of the lock, water ran downhill under the floor of the lock. It bubbled up gently into the lock from holes drilled in the floor. The lock filled with water and lifted the waiting ship. After the ship passed through the lock, a valve at the lower end was opened. The water drained out.

The locks were finished in June 1913. Then Gatun Dam's spillway gates were closed. Gatun Lake began to rise. President Wilson pushed the button that flooded the Culebra Cut on October 10. On August 15, 1914, the Panama Canal opened for business.

EXPLORE ONLINE

Chapter Three describes how the Panama Canal locks were built. The website below provides an animation of a ship passing through a set of locks. How does it help you better understand what a lock is and how it works?

HOW LOCKS WORK
abdocorelibrary.com/engineering-panama-canal

CHAPTER FOUR

THE PANAMA CANAL TODAY

The original locks and channels of the Panama Canal are more than 100 years old. Despite their age, they work almost perfectly. In September 2010, the one millionth ship passed through the canal. Today, the canal hosts more than 30 ships a day. It provides thousands of jobs for local residents.

MAINTENANCE

The canal requires regular upkeep to run smoothly. This includes maintaining the locks

The Panama Canal remains vital to global travel and trade.

and machinery. Mudslides during rainy times continue to fill channels and lakes with mud and rocks. They must be dredged often to keep them clear.

Over the last century, ships have become bigger. Many became too big to fit through the Panama Canal. For this reason, Panama began a major expansion project in 2007. It was one of the world's biggest engineering projects.

MAJOR EXPANSION

The channels at each sea entrance were widened. The channels

> **PERSPECTIVES**
> ### PANAMA GAINS CONTROL
> Panama gained full control of the canal in 1999. Today, the canal is Panama's largest source of money. Ships pay to use the canal. The largest cargo ships pay up to $1 million for one passage. The canal earns Panama more than $2 billion per year. The money funds projects such as education, buildings, and roads. Panama also is responsible for the protection of the entire canal watershed. The Panama Canal is an important source of jobs and pride for the people of Panama.

The upgraded canal infrastructure can be used by huge ships.

also were deepened. That is because bigger ships sit deeper in the water. The channels across Gatun Lake and through the cut were widened and deepened too.

Gatun Lake was raised to 89 feet (27 m). Gatun Dam was made stronger to handle the bigger lake.

A third lane for boat traffic was added at each end of the canal. This lane is big enough for much larger ships. The third lane has new, larger locks. The gates on these new locks slide inside the wall rather than swing closed. The project was finished in the summer of 2016.

When the original canal and locks project was finished, it was considered the greatest engineering marvel of its time. Advances in electrical engineering, technology, and medicine resulted from

> **SAVING WATER**
>
> Each time a ship passes through the original lock system, 52 million gallons (197 million L) of freshwater rush into the sea. The new locks finished in 2016 were designed to recycle and save water. The locks are connected to reserve basins. These basins collect some of the water each time a ship passes. The water in the basin is then reused for the next ship. The new locks use 48 million gallons (182 million L) of freshwater.

its construction. The expansion project was another great feat of engineering and technology. The Panama Canal is now ready for its next 100 years of service.

FURTHER EVIDENCE

Chapter Four summarizes the recent expansion project of the Panama Canal. What was one of the main points of the chapter? What evidence is included to support this point? The website at the link below features a short video about the project. Does it support the information provided in the chapter? Does it offer new information?

A NEW EXPERIENCE—THE PANAMA CANAL
abdocorelibrary.com/engineering-panama-canal

FAST FACTS

- The Isthmus of Panama is the narrowest strip of land separating the Atlantic and Pacific Oceans.

- The Panama Canal shortens the distance ships must travel from the Atlantic Ocean to the Pacific Ocean by thousands of miles. This saves weeks of travel time.

- The Panama Canal is approximately 50 miles (81 km) long.

- People came from all over the world to work on the Panama Canal, including the United States, Europe, Asia, Latin America, and the Caribbean.

- Dr. William Gorgas developed a plan for ridding the Canal Zone of yellow fever and significantly reducing the cases of malaria. His ideas later helped prevent tropical diseases across the world.

- The Gatun Dam was the largest earthen dam in the world when finished.

- Gatun Lake, which formed behind Gatun Dam, was the largest artificial lake in the world at the time it was formed.

- The Culebra Cut was the largest excavation project ever attempted at the time.

- The Panama Canal locks fill and empty with water powered by gravity.

- The locks on the Panama Canal use hydroelectric power.
- Americans began building the canal in 1904 and finished in 1914.
- The lock expansion project was begun in 2009 and finished in 2016.
- The largest ships pay tolls of up to $1 million to use the new locks on the Panama Canal.

STOP AND THINK

Tell the Tale
Chapter Three describes some of the difficult conditions faced by some of the people who lived and worked in the Panama Canal Zone. Imagine you are a laborer. Write 200 words about your experience. How would you feel about the Panama Canal?

Say What?
Studying the engineering and construction of the Panama Canal can mean learning a lot of new vocabulary. Find five words in this book you had never heard before. Use a dictionary to find out what they mean. Then write the meanings in your own words and use each word in a new sentence.

Take a Stand
Throughout his presidency, Theodore Roosevelt defended his actions in Panama. Some people said he helped the rebellion. Do you think Roosevelt's actions in Panama were justified? Why or why not?

Why Do I Care?

You might never travel through the Panama Canal. But food you eat and products you use likely do. Is it important that the canal be maintained and improved? How might the world be different without the canal?

GLOSSARY

canal
a long waterway built by humans that links two bodies of water

infrastructure
the basic equipment and structures that a project or community needs to function properly

insecticide
a substance used to kill insects

isthmus
a narrow strip of land that connects two larger pieces of land and has water on both sides

lock
a device that raises and lowers ships between stretches of water of different levels on a canal

spillway
a structure that provides a safe release of flood waters from a dam to the river downstream

turbine
an engine that provides energy when falling water turns a wheel with blades

watershed
an entire area of land that drains into a single river

ONLINE RESOURCES

To learn more about the Panama Canal, visit our free resource websites below.

Visit **abdocorelibrary.com** for free Common Core resources for teachers and students, including vetted activities, multimedia, and booklinks, for deeper subject comprehension.

Visit **abdobooklinks.com** for free additional online weblinks for further learning. These links are routinely monitored and updated to provide the most current information available.

LEARN MORE

Benoit, Peter. *The Panama Canal.* New York: Children's Press, 2014.

Pascal, Janet. *What Is the Panama Canal?* New York: Grosset & Dunlap, 2014.

INDEX

Bucyrus steam shovel, 18, 21, 28, 31

canal plan, 14, 18, 20–22, 23, 25, 26, 31

Canal Zone, 10, 14, 16, 34

Chagres River, 20, 21, 22, 23, 26, 28

concrete, 26, 31, 32

Culebra Cut, 7, 20, 25, 28, 30–31, 35

disease, 7, 14, 16–17, 30

dredges, 32, 38

expansion project, 38–41

explosives, 5, 21, 30

French canal project, 7–8, 13, 14, 21

Gatun Dam, 20, 22, 25, 26–28, 30, 32, 34, 35, 40

Goethals, George, 25

Gorgas, William, 14, 16–17

infrastructure, 14, 17–18, 30

Isthmus of Panama, 6–7, 21

lock canal, 21, 22, 23, 25

locks, 20, 21, 22, 25, 26, 31–32, 34–35, 37, 40

maintenance, 23, 37–38

mosquitoes, 16–17

mudslides, 21, 26, 30–31, 38

Panama Canal Treaty, 8, 10

railroads, 7, 13, 18, 21, 28–31

Republic of Panama, 8, 11, 38

Roosevelt, Theodore, 8, 10, 11, 22

safety, 14, 16–17, 28, 30

sea-level canal, 7, 13–14, 21–22, 23, 25

spoil, 28, 30, 32

Stevens, John, 14, 16, 17–18, 22, 23

Wallace, John, 13–14

Wilson, Woodrow, 5, 35

workers, 7, 10, 14, 16, 17, 26, 28, 30–31, 32

About the Author

Yvette LaPierre lives in North Dakota with her family, two dogs, and two crested geckos. She once traveled through locks on the Mississippi River near Minneapolis, Minnesota.